Break the Money Circuit
Our Guide to Rewiring Energy, Flow, and Financial Freedom

How to Use This Book

This book began with a discovery: the financial system we're born into isn't just a system of dollars and cents — it's built like an electrical circuit board. Quite literally. Once I saw that, it unlocked something deeper: money is energy. Currency is an electric current.

I don't earn energy. I am energy. When I began aligning with my true energetic self, I stopped burning out chasing power — and started tapping into it. I became my own lighthouse. I became a power station.

And here's the truth: you can too.

This book is broken into fifty Sparks, each short, punchy, and practical. Every Spark is designed to resonate and ignite something inside you.

In the early Sparks, I speak in first person — because I'm not above this. I am inside this work, rewiring myself alongside you.

In the middle Sparks, the voice shifts to you — to challenge, invite, and mirror your own patterns.

By the final Sparks, we land in we/us — because by then, the journey is no longer just mine or yours. It's ours. And together, we are stronger, more electric, more alive.

Each Spark follows a simple pattern:

CHARGE — a perspective shift to help you see differently

FLOW — a deeper exploration of the idea

SWITCH — a small action or intention to anchor the concept

Read them in order or skip around — but if you follow these Sparks from beginning to end, you will feel a shift not just in your thinking, but in the way you carry your energy.

The Spark That Started It All

We are born live wired. Every current in our life — money, purpose, energy — is already there, waiting for us to remember how to direct it.

Through years of study and practice, I discovered a common theme running through the stories of every great success: success is not an accident, but a program. A way of thinking and acting that can be installed, like a code.

And here's the spark that changed everything for me: crystal — the most abundant mineral on Earth — is the same material used to program the microchips in our modern world. Crystal holds and transmits information. It creates the foundation for everything from our phones to our computers.

If we can program a crystal, why not program ourselves?

We, too, are conductors, built to channel and direct energy. We can reprogram our own grid — by grounding into connection, refining our patterns, and living on purpose.

I wrote this book to help you reconnect to your true energetic self, both inside your spirit and out in the world.

Fifty Sparks, each designed to rewire how you relate to wealth, energy, and your sense of purpose.

Read them one per day, or all at once. These Sparks will live with you, because they live in you.

Stay in the circuit.

WAKE UP TO THE CIRCUIT

We don't just live in a system.
We carry it inside us.

SPARKS ~ ONE to TEN

This section explores how energy is the real currency of life — and how money, time, and productivity are simply modern forms of how energy gets exchanged.

Recognizing this flow is the first step to using it with intention.

These Sparks will help you remember: money doesn't power you. You power the system.

Money isn't power
—you are.

SPARK 1:

I was born **Plugged In**

I didn't join the
system—
I just woke up inside it.

⚡CHARGE

I didn't come into this world empty. I arrived wired for connection, creativity, and flow. But from the start, we've been plugged into systems — family, school, money — that began shaping how we channel that energy.

⚡FLOW

Everyday life teaches me to think energy is something to chase: grades, approval, success, wealth. But it's not. It's something we are. Watch any kid light up when they play — that's pure current. Somewhere along the way, we forget we're already carrying the charge.

⚡SWITCH

Stop asking: Where do I get more energy?
Start asking: Where am I leaking it? Where am I blocking it?
We're already plugged in — my job now is to clear the line.

SPARK 2:

I'm not in the grid
I Am the Grid

I am not riding the current.
I am carrying the current.

⚡ CHARGE

I don't just exist in the system—I power it. My presence fuels conversations, spaces, teams. I'm not a passenger. I'm part of the circuit.

⚡ FLOW

I feel it—when I shift a room, when I lift or lower the charge around me. I've seen my energy ripple outward, even when I didn't mean to. I'm not separate from the system. I am the signal.

⚡ SWITCH

Every interaction is a circuit. I choose what I power. I manage my current like it matters—because it does.

SPARK 3:

I am **Energy**

I'm not a battery —
I'm the charge itself.

ϟ CHARGE

I'm not holding energy — I am energy. My thoughts, emotions, and presence flow like current. I don't "run out of charge" — I shift, pulse, recharge.

ϟ FLOW

I feel it when something sparks me — or drains me. That buzz in my gut, the static in my mind, the charge in my chest — it's real. I'm not just alive; I'm electric.

ϟ SWITCH

I'm not a fuel tank running on fumes. I am the current. When I tune in, I don't run out — I move, flow, amplify.

SPARK 4:

Money Moves
I Make It Flow

Currency isn't power.
It's plumbing.

⚡ CHARGE

I used to believe money was the source of my power. But money only moves what's already flowing in me. It routes energy, but it doesn't create it. That realization changed everything.

⚡ FLOW

Money is like pipes in a house. Without pressure behind them, those pipes stay empty or clogged. You can jiggle the handle all day, but if there's no water pressure, nothing moves. Money is just the conduit — the real force begins in me.

⚡ SWITCH

I will stop obsessing over the pipes. I'll build my own water pressure, my own current, my own purpose. That current will flow through money — but it starts with me.

SPARK 5:

Power is Directed— **Not Earned**

Work isn't the source.
Alignment is.

CHARGE

I was raised to believe power comes from hard work alone. Push harder. Stay later. Prove myself. But effort without alignment is just noise – wasted current.

FLOW

Real power doesn't come from endless motion. It comes from knowing where I'm going, and why. Alignment turns every action into a focused beam of energy. When I line up with what truly matters, even a small effort can move mountains.

SWITCH

I will stop trying to hustle my way to power. I will align first – then act. Energy follows clarity.

SPARK 6:

Not a consumer
A Conduit

I don't hold energy—
I move it.

CHARGE

It's easy to fall into the trap of consuming: money, media, validation. I was taught to gather, collect, and store energy — as if I could run out. But I'm not a storage tank. I'm a conduit.

FLOW

When I try to absorb everything — ideas, emotions, expectations — I get overwhelmed. Flow disappears. But when I let energy move through me, everything aligns. A clean conduit doesn't block, it transmits.

SWITCH

I will stop hoarding energy. I will stay open, letting the current pass through without getting stuck. That's real power.

SPARK 7:

Scarcity is a **Circuit Problem**

If life feels scarce,
check the wiring.

⚡ CHARGE

Scarcity isn't solved by chasing more—it's solved by rerouting flow. When things feel tight, it's usually my old programming clamping down the current. I don't need more to feel safe; I need to rewire how I circulate what I already have.

⚡ FLOW

I've gripped jobs, relationships, and decisions out of fear there wouldn't be enough. I've mistaken survival mode for truth, shrinking my flow and hoarding energy like it might vanish. But scarcity is often just conditioning—a loop I was taught, not a law of nature.

⚡ SWITCH

I stop chasing more and check the wiring. The quickest reset? Gratitude. Every time I recognize what's already flowing, I strengthen the circuit and invite more power through.

SPARK 8:

Abundance is an **Open Circuit**

Abundance isn't
more—
it's momentum.

CHARGE

Abundance isn't about having everything—it's about letting everything move. When my energy flows freely, opportunities find me. Alignment creates access.

FLOW

I've felt abundance in deep conversations, creative sparks, and those moments when everything just clicks—not just in my bank account. The less I grip, the more it grows. When I release the choke points, I see: the current is always ready to flow.

SWITCH

Abundance isn't stockpiling—it's circulation. When I keep my circuit clear and my energy moving, life plugs in around me. Flow invites more flow.

SPARK 9:

I Am Not Tired
I Am Leaking

Most burnout is just unplugged energy.

CHARGE

I've blamed exhaustion on not having enough energy. But most of the time, I'm not truly empty – I'm leaking power into the wrong places.

FLOW

I've scrolled when I should've rested. I've said yes when I meant no. I've stayed in rooms that dimmed me. That's not burnout–it's running on someone else's current. Disconnection disguised as discipline.

SWITCH

I will check for leaks in my time, relationships, and thoughts. I will patch those leaks and plug back into what actually charges me. When I reconnect to what matters, my power surges back online.

SPARK 10:

I Recharge **By Design**

Rest is a blueprint,
not accident.

CHARGE

I thought stopping was enough to recharge. But rest without structure is just collapse. True recovery needs intention.

FLOW

A power grid doesn't recover through random downtime; it resets through deliberate patterns, recalibrating its flow and protecting its circuits. In the same way, I need patterns that rebuild me on purpose. When I weave intention into how I pause, I don't just rest — I restore.

SWITCH

I will choose one simple recharge pattern to anchor each day. Not a rescue — a design. That is how I keep my power flowing. Gratitude, breath, boundaries, movement — these aren't luxuries. They are anchors for change and stability.

SECTION TWO

KNOW YOUR HARDWARE

Understand the system.
Control the flow.

SPARKS ~ ELEVEN to TWENTY

We're not just powered by energy—we're built from it. The hardware inside us runs like a power grid: circuits, regulators, resistors, breakers. Every reaction and pattern flows through that system.

This section names the parts and shows you how they work—because the moment we understand how we're wired, we can stop running on autopilot and start directing the current with precision.

This is not theory.
It's your wiring diagram.

SPARK 11:

Voltage = **Want**

Desire is pressure—
it builds until I move.

⚡ CHARGE

Want isn't weakness—it's stored energy. Every desire is voltage building up inside me, asking for release. The stronger the want, the higher the charge. It's not teasing me—it's pushing me toward action.

⚡ FLOW

I've called my wants selfish. I've waited for permission or felt frustrated when nothing moved. But that tension? It's not frustration—it's potential energy, looking for an outlet. Voltage doesn't ask—it finds a path.

⚡ SWITCH

I stop judging what I want and start translating it. Want is the current's first signal—and I'm done pretending I don't hear it.

SPARK 12:

Current = **Presence**

Flow only happens
when I'm here for it.

⚡ CHARGE

Current doesn't flow through memory, plans, or performance. It only flows through presence. The moment I arrive fully—mind, body, energy—I activate the circuit.

⚡ FLOW

I've done days on autopilot. Nodded through conversations without listening, while my mind wandered off. That's not flow. That's disconnection dressed as discipline.

⚡ SWITCH

If I want flow, I have to plug in. My power lives in presence. I practice coming back with one breath, one foot on the floor, one look away from the screen. The power lives here, not later.

SPARK 13:

Resistance = **Feedback**

Resistance rises when something real is near.

⚡ CHARGE

Resistance isn't weakness — it's a compass, pointing toward the thing I was meant to do. Creative energy attracts friction. That's not failure — it's physics.

⚡ FLOW

I've felt resistance most when I'm about to level up. When I sit down to build, speak, change, or create — there it is. Every distraction, every delay, every doubt. Resistance tests my clarity and commitment. It shows me I'm close to what matters.

⚡ SWITCH

I will treat resistance like a starting bell, not a stop sign. When it shows up, I'll lean in and smile, knowing I'm close to what matters most.

SPARK 14:

Ground = **Safety**

Stability isn't stillness—
it's strategy.

⚡ CHARGE

Every electrical system needs a ground—it's the only thing keeping excess energy from becoming destruction. Without a place to safely discharge, current builds pressure until something arcs, melts, or blows.

⚡ FLOW

Quartz runs your computer. It holds memory, stabilizes energy, and grounds digital systems. Nature made it abundant and programmable. Maybe grounding isn't spiritual fluff—it's how complex systems—including me—stay safe under charge.

⚡ SWITCH

The more I ground, the more energy I can carry without frying the system. I charge my foundation so I can hold more power. Sand, dirt—even asphalt—are packed with quartz. Go touch it with intention. Stability isn't retreat—it's infrastructure.

SPARK 15:

Conductor = **Clarity**

The cleanest path
carries the most power.

⚡ CHARGE

A conductor doesn't create energy—it carries it. In a circuit, it moves current cleanly from point to point without losing charge. When I'm clear and grounded, I become the wire—and the one holding the map.

⚡ FLOW

I've overloaded my system by carrying everything at once—no direction, just noise. Tasks, emotions, expectations—all tangled like crossed wires. But when I pause and choose the current that's truly mine, energy flows. Power isn't in doing more—it's in knowing what to move.

⚡ SWITCH

I clear the signal. I drop what isn't mine to carry. I choose one current and move it clean. Because the more precise the path, the more power gets through.

SPARK 16:

Capacitor = **Capacity**

Rest is a
voltage strategy.

CHARGE

I thought pushing harder was the only way to expand my capacity.
But I was wrong. Pauses don't shrink my power — they build it.

FLOW

Like a capacitor, I can hold energy and release it at the right moment. When I store wisely, I grow my ability to handle greater charge — without burning out. It's not weakness to pause — it's strategic wiring.

SWITCH

I will trust the stillness that helps me build voltage. I will hold power with care, then release it when the moment is right.

SPARK 17:

Amplifier = **Voice**

My energy gets louder when I speak it clearly.

⚡ CHARGE

An amplifier boosts a signal without changing its truth. It doesn't scream—it strengthens. My voice doesn't need to be perfect or loud to carry power. It needs to be clean.

⚡ FLOW

I've dulled my voice to stay agreeable. I've overexplained to feel safe. But an unclear signal confuses the system. When I speak from alignment—without distortion or apology—my energy cuts through noise.

⚡ SWITCH

My voice is how energy moves through others. The cleaner the message, the farther it travels. Don't boost the noise—boost the signal.

SPARK 18:

Fuse = **Limits**

Breakdowns aren't failure—they're feedback.

CHARGE

A fuse isn't fragile—it's designed to break first. When the current spikes, the fuse interrupts the flow to protect everything else. Ask any electrician—meltdowns cost more than fuses.

FLOW

I've ignored my limits, pushed past the hum, overridden the flickering lights. Then I wondered why I snapped. A blown fuse doesn't mean I'm broken. It means something needs rewiring.

SWITCH

I stop treating limits like enemies. I install them with intention. Because when I don't choose where to break—I break somewhere I didn't choose.

SPARK 19:

Circuit = **Boundaries**

Without a loop,
nothing flows.

CHARGE

A circuit only works when the loop is closed. Boundaries don't block energy—they define the path it moves through. An open loop isn't freedom. It's dysfunction.

FLOW

I've said yes to everything, kept all the channels open, and still felt drained. Because energy doesn't flow without structure—it leaks. Boundaries aren't barriers. They're the reason power reaches its destination.

SWITCH

I close the loop. I define what's in and what's out. I stop running an open system and start building a stronger circuit. Boundaries aren't rejection—they're design.

SPARK 20:

Power = **Purpose**

If I don't know who I am, nothing powers right.

⚡ CHARGE

Every circuit has a source. Without it, wires are just potential. Identity is the voltage behind the system. When I forget who I am, I hand my power to things that can't carry it.

⚡ FLOW

I've burned out trying to run systems that weren't mine—jobs, relationships, ideals. I looked busy, but I wasn't plugged into anything real. When I root back into my core wiring, energy flows better everywhere else.

⚡ SWITCH

I stop outsourcing power to titles, roles, and approval. I reconnect to who I am—not who I've been performing as. Identity isn't a costume. It's the original current.

SECTION THREE

ROLES ON THE GRID

You don't just use energy—
you move it.

SPARKS ~ TWENTY-ONE to THIRTY

Whenever we say "I Am," we're not just naming who we are—we're shaping who we're becoming. It's not a title. It's a function. A role we can step into, shift out of, and return to as the current demands.

This section isn't about identity or personality. It's about how we show up in the grid. Sometimes we lead the charge. Sometimes we ground it. Sometimes we just hold the current steady.

Your role isn't fixed.
It revolves and evolves.

SPARK 21:

I Am the Valve
Not The Block

Releasing is wiser than breaking.

⚡ CHARGE

I thought holding on made me strong. But clinging to lost love, lost dreams, or old identities doesn't heal me — it jams me up.

⚡ FLOW

A valve releases pressure so the whole system stays safe. Loss builds pressure too — grief, disappointment, heartbreak. If I never let it move through, it hardens and locks down everything inside me.

⚡ SWITCH

I will allow loss and change to move through me, not freeze inside me. I will open the valve so my heart can breathe again. That is how I keep my power alive.

SPARK 22:

I Am a Resistor

The Regulator

Slowing the current isn't weakness—it's what keeps the circuit safe.

ϟ CHARGE

A resistor doesn't block energy—it controls it. It protects the system by slowing the current just enough to keep things from frying.

ϟ FLOW

Resistors show up when tension spikes, tempers rise, or pressure builds. They hold the pace, anchor the circuit, and keep the whole thing from going up in smoke.

ϟ SWITCH

When the energy starts racing, regulate it—lower your voice, slow your breath, ground your stance. Cool heads aren't weak—they're wired right. Not all heroes charge ahead—some of us hit the brakes.

SPARK 23:

I Am Filtering **The Frequency**

Not every current deserves my airtime.

⚡ CHARGE

I've let every voice, every worry, every hot take rush through me — as if they all deserved a slot. But not every program gets to broadcast on my channel.

⚡ FLOW

My energy is precious bandwidth. A filter isn't rejection — it's protection. By choosing what signals I allow, I keep my current clean and my system stable.

⚡ SWITCH

I will decide what gets airtime and what gets muted. I have the power to change the channel, leaving behind the programs I grew up with but outgrew.

SPARK 24:

I Am a Transformer

The Adapter

The right energy at the right level changes everything.

⚡ CHARGE

A transformer doesn't create energy—it adjusts it. It steps voltage up or down so the system can use it without blowing out or burning up.

⚡ FLOW

Transformers shift the vibe. They amplify when momentum needs a push, and ground things when it's too much. They don't force—they calibrate.

⚡ SWITCH

Before you react, ask: does this moment need more charge... or less? Transform the energy to match the moment. Right voltage, right outcome. Become the voltage whisperer.

SPARK 25:

I Am the Voice
The Amplifier

What gets amplified
gets heard.

CHARGE

An amplifier doesn't judge the signal—it just makes it louder. Whatever comes in gets projected out, bigger and harder to ignore.

FLOW

Amplifiers raise more than volume—they raise momentum, emotion, and meaning. But they can also blow up drama, fear, or noise. What gets picked up gets broadcast.

SWITCH

So I don't just boost what's loudest. I tune in. I choose the signal I want to scale—because whatever I amplify becomes the message.

SPARK 26:

I Am the Rewriter
The Inverter

Energy doesn't
disappear—
it changes form.

⚡ CHARGE

An inverter doesn't stop energy. It flips it. It converts current from one form to another to meet the moment's needs.

⚡ FLOW

Inverters can turn tension into fuel—or fuel into frenzy. They don't block charge—they rewire it midstream.

⚡ SWITCH

Flipping energy is power. But flip unconsciously, and you create chaos. Redirect it with intention—or get rerouted by it.

SPARK 27:

I Am a Relay
The Switch

Not every action
needs force—some
just need permission.

⚡CHARGE

A relay doesn't store power. It responds to a signal and completes the circuit. One click—and energy moves.

⚡FLOW

Relays respond instantly. No hesitation. No delay.When the signal's clear, they connect. Fast, clean, done.

⚡SWITCH

Power isn't always pressure. Sometimes it's timing. Real strength is knowing when to click in—and when to stay open.

SPARK 28:

I Am the Protector
The Fuse

A fuse doesn't fail—
it saves the system.

⚡ CHARGE

A fuse is built to break first. When energy surges beyond safe limits, it takes the hit—so everything else stays intact.

⚡ FLOW

Fuses absorb what others can't. They interrupt the current to prevent a full system collapse. It's not self-sabotage if it saves the circuit.

⚡ SWITCH

Breaking isn't weakness. Sometimes, it's the most protective move you can make—for you, and for everyone downstream.

SPARK 29:

I Am a Stabilizer

The Ground

Power without grounding is a threat.

⚡ CHARGE

Grounding gives excess energy somewhere to go. It stabilizes the system, protects the current, and keeps a surge from becoming destruction.

⚡ FLOW

Grounds show up as the steady presence in chaos. They absorb emotional spikes, defuse tension, and keep systems from collapsing under pressure. Stillness is an active force.

⚡ SWITCH

Strength isn't just generating power—it's creating safe places for energy to land. Sometimes stability is the spark that saves the circuit. Grounding isn't retreat—it's voltage insurance.

SPARK 30:

I Am the Source
The Power Station

Real power isn't
borrowed—
it's generated.

CHARGE

A power station doesn't wait for energy—it makes it. It pulls from heat, pressure, and raw materials, then converts it into steady, usable current.

FLOW

Power stations light cities, move industries, and fuel entire systems. In the same way, the energy we generate drives our relationships, our work, and our impact.

SWITCH

Energy isn't handed to us. It starts when we choose to create—not wait. If you're always waiting for the spark, you'll miss your chance to ignite.

SECTION FOUR

SPOTTING SHORT CIRCUITS

When I don't guard my flow, I lose it.

SPARKS ~ THIRTY-ONE to FORTY

This section maps the traps that scatter energy, hijack attention, and reroute momentum.

The drains are subtle—loops, leaks, distractions—but their impact is real.

They pull current from the circuit that's meant to move our life forward.

Small glitches are worth big fixes.

Every glitch has a source.
Let's find ours, together.

SPARK 31:

Energy Leak
Tiny Drains

We barely notice
what drains us most.

⚡ CHARGE

A circuit doesn't die from one big surge. It fades from a slow, silent leak. Bit by bit, the power bleeds out.

⚡ FLOW

Leaks show up in tiny habits—unfinished tasks, overthinking, low-level dread, resentment that simmers. Nothing dramatic. Just steady loss.

⚡ SWITCH

Stop the small leaks—habits, distractions, avoidances. Fix what we can fix and release what we can't—through prayer, trust, and support. That's how we keep the current clean.

SPARK 32:

Overload

Too Much Current

Every meltdown starts with ignoring the limits.

CHARGE

A circuit isn't weak because it trips—it's wise. When the current gets too strong, it shuts down to protect what's left.

FLOW

Overload doesn't always announce itself. It looks like running late, rushing through, saying yes out of habit, or trying to carry what was never yours. It melts slow—until it snaps.

SWITCH

Overload isn't a badge of honor. Set load limits early. Say no sooner. A system that's always maxed out isn't strong—it's exposed. If we don't schedule discharge, life will schedule a meltdown.

SPARK 33:

False Wiring
Wrong Blueprint

I can't run my power through someone else's design.

⚡CHARGE

False wiring doesn't start with fear. It starts with loyalty—trusting the people who handed me the blueprint. It feels like love, duty, or survival… until it doesn't.

⚡FLOW

Staying wired to someone else's design doesn't win peace—it drains power. Reclaiming energy means rerouting to the current I was born to carry.

⚡SWITCH

Stop chasing what looks right and start building what feels electric.
Energy flows best when we follow the circuit made for us. See the dead-end? Take the U-turn.

SPARK 34:

Noise Hijacked Attention

Even powerful signals get lost in static.

CHARGE

Noise doesn't crash the system—it confuses it. It scrambles clarity, buries focus, and scatters even strong energy. The result? A circuit still powered—but misfiring.

FLOW

Hijacked attention looks like endless inputs—scrolling, alerts, hot takes, opinions—layered until we can't hear ourselves think. It's not weakness. It's interference.

SWITCH

Clearing the noise isn't a luxury—it's how power gets restored. Cut the static. Reclaim the signal. Our focus is voltage. Silence isn't empty—it's where our real power finally gets through.

SPARK 35:

Loop Fail

Echo Chambers

What repeats long enough starts to sound like truth.

⚡ CHARGE

A feedback loop traps energy. Instead of moving forward, the current circles itself—growing louder, but going nowhere new.

⚡ FLOW

Loops show up in familiar voices cheering for safe choices, low effort, and comfortable patterns. Sometimes kindness becomes a cage—trapping current instead of moving it.

⚡ SWITCH

Comfort doesn't mean we are right—it means we are on repeat. Get outside the echo. Interrupt the pattern. Progress doesn't cheer—it challenges. If no one's pushing back, you might be parked.

SPARK 36:

Disconnection
Cut From Source

Effort without connection burns out the strongest circuits.

⚡ CHARGE

When a system loses connection to its source, it still looks intact—but current stops moving. Energy fades. Momentum dies. No amount of effort can force a flow that isn't there.

⚡ FLOW

Disconnection doesn't always look like failure. It looks like trying hard… and feeling nothing. Long days. Numb conversations. Silent goals.

⚡ SWITCH

Reconnection isn't magic. It's a move. Step back. Reset. Rewire. I will reach for reconnection before I declare myself powerless. Even the smallest spark can restart the flow.

SPARK 37:

Parasitic Load

The Hidden Drain

Not everyone plugged into my life is adding power.

CHARGE

A parasitic load pulls energy even when the system looks like it's off. It drains current slowly, quietly, and constantly—weakening the whole grid over time.

FLOW

These loads show up as toxic relationships, fake loyalty, one-sided obligations, and emotional debts that never repay. They don't crash the system—they just bleed it dry, unnoticed.

SWITCH

I will pull the plugs that drain me and trust I have enough current of my own to thrive. Releasing these hidden drains is how I reclaim my flow.
We are not rude — we're rewiring.

SPARK 38:

Crossed Wires

The Misfires

Scattered energy
can’t spark anything.

CHARGE

Crossed wires confuse the system. Signals collide, cancel out, or short before they land. Even strong current gets lost when the pathways are tangled.

FLOW

It shows up as fractured focus, scattered commitments, and chasing too many goals at once. It feels like action—but nothing connects, and nothing completes.

SWITCH

I will pause and untangle the overload, knowing multitasking can cross my wires faster than a toddler with a box of Christmas lights. One clear connection at a time rebuilds my circuit, stronger and steadier.

SPARK 39:

Faulty Loop
The Frozen Circuit

When energy gets trapped, it burns itself out.

CHARGE

A faulty loop traps current in place. It doesn't move forward—it just spins, draining the system with every cycle.

FLOW

We know the feeling: emotional flashbacks, regrets on repeat, loyalty to old pain. The circuit fires and fires—but never moves past the memory.

SWITCH

Breaking the loop takes a jolt of intention. Old currents don't clear with time—they clear with courage. Loops lie to keep us stuck. Reroute, and break free.

SPARK 40:

Dead Outlet **Waiting for a Charge**

Waiting for outside power leaves the circuit dead.

CHARGE

A dead outlet looks like part of the system—but it doesn't move energy.
It sits, wired in but empty, waiting for something external to give it life.

FLOW

Dead outlets show up when we wait for rescue—the perfect job, perfect partner, or perfect timing to finally light us up. But waiting doesn't create power. It drains it.

SWITCH

The current doesn't come from outside. We either generate it—or stay unplugged. We will stop waiting to be powered. Hope isn't a power source. Action is..

SECTION FIVE

FLOW AND FREEDOM

Freedom is a current I build, not a prize I win

SPARKS ~ FORTY-ONE to FIFTY

This section is about rebuilding momentum with clean circuits, steady currents, and real connection to the source.

Not every wire deserves to stay.

Not every current deserves to flow through me.

Flow isn't forced. It's built.

When I honor the current,
the current carries me.

SPARK 41:

Clean Circuit **Clear Current**

Flow isn't hustle—
it's hygiene.

⚡ CHARGE

A clean circuit doesn't force current—it allows it. No blockages. No cross-signals. No hidden drains. When the wiring's right, the current moves naturally.

⚡ FLOW

When I push too hard, I confuse pressure with progress. Real flow isn't about effort—it's about clearing friction, re-aligning signal, and letting the energy move.

⚡ SWITCH

I clean the corrosion, tighten the wires, and let the power run clear. Flow isn't stronger when I push harder. It's smoother when I clear the path.

SPARK 42:

Right Load
Right Flow

I don't need more energy.
I need the right load for my current.

ϟ CHARGE

Every circuit is built for a specific load. Too much current overheats it. Too little, and nothing moves. Flow isn't about force—it's about fit.

ϟ FLOW

Saying yes to everything shorts my system.But when I match my energy to what actually matters, everything moves cleaner—and faster.

ϟ SWITCH

I move faster when I drop the weight that was never mine to carry.
Right voltage. Right current. Right outcome. Alignment isn't luxury—it's velocity.

SPARK 43:

Conductors Only **High-Flow Connections**

Friction is not chemistry—it's a wiring issue.

CHARGE

A true conductor doesn't block or resist—it carries current cleanly. The right connections don't weigh me down. They pick up the signal and move it farther, faster.

FLOW

When I'm stuck explaining, proving, or dragging dead weight, the current slows. The right people and projects don't just keep up—they amplify the signal.

SWITCH

I don't bond with blocks.I build with conductors The right connections don't drain me—they move me faster. If I have to force the flow, it's not a connection—it's a clog.

SPARK 44:

Surge Capacity
Hold More Power

Growth doesn't just need more energy—it needs a system that can handle it.

ϟ CHARGE

A surge of power can light up a system—or fry it. Without capacity, more energy just creates overload. Strength isn't wanting more. It's being ready to carry it.

ϟ FLOW

When I stretch myself too thin without upgrading my systems, I short-circuit. But when I reinforce my boundaries, habits, and support structures, I can hold bigger flows without burning out.

ϟ SWITCH

I don't just chase bigger energy. I build the capacity to carry it—clean, steady, and strong. The current will rise. I rise with it—or I blow a fuse.

SPARK 45:

Rewire for Freedom
Build New Paths

Freedom isn't
escape—
it's energy flowing
through new circuits.

CHARGE

Rewiring isn't just fixing the past. It's creating new routes for current to travel. Without fresh pathways, even the strongest energy gets trapped in old loops.

FLOW

When I build new habits, form better connections, and reshape my beliefs, I create flow that can carry more of what matters. Freedom doesn't come from breaking away. It comes from building systems that move me forward.

SWITCH

I don't just cut old wires. I build new circuits that carry my power—clean, open, and free. Breaking free is good. Rewiring forward is better.

SPARK 46:

Adaptive Systems **Move Through Resistance**

Resistance isn't a wall—it's proof the current matters.

CHARGE

An adaptive system doesn't freeze at resistance. It redirects, recalibrates, or flexes to keep the current alive. Rigidity snaps. Adaptability flows.

FLOW

Sometimes resistance is external—delays, doubt, challenge. Sometimes it's internal—fear, perfectionism, distraction. Either way, I don't have to force it. I can shift, realign, and keep moving. Resistance shows up where it matters most.

SWITCH

I stop treating Resistance like a warning—it's a milestone. It means I'm near something meaningful, which is why the distractions show up—I turn Resistance into alignment, and friction into forward motion.

SPARK 47:

Signal Integrity
Stay True

The real power?
Uninterrupted flow.

⚡ CHARGE

In a circuit, integrity means the message moves clean—no distortion, no interference, no signal loss. Without it, even strong currents break down before they arrive.

⚡ FLOW

When life gets loud, chaotic, or distracting, I don't need to amplify the noise. I protect the core: my mission, my message, my direction.
That's what keeps the current true.

⚡ SWITCH

I don't shout louder. I tune sharper. The clearest current always cuts through. While others scream static, I broadcast purpose.

SPARK 48:

Continuous Flow
How Power Grows

Power builds when energy stays in motion.

⚡CHARGE

In an electrical system, continuous flow keeps energy stable and efficient.
Stops, surges, and interruptions waste power and strain the circuit.
Smooth, steady current delivers the most over time.

⚡FLOW

When I stay consistent—showing up, moving forward, staying in rhythm—my energy compounds. It's not about bursts of intensity. It's about the quiet strength that builds when I keep moving.

⚡SWITCH

I'm not chasing lightning—I'm laying down wire. One clear step at a time, I keep the current alive. I power through Resistance. Steady rhythm becomes unstoppable power.

SPARK 49:

Signal Source

Lead By Example

A steady signal
becomes a point of
alignment
for others.

⚡CHARGE

In a system, the signal source sets the rhythm. It broadcasts consistent current that the rest of the circuit syncs to. Without it, everything drifts or destabilizes.

⚡FLOW

When I'm aligned—with purpose, clarity, and conviction—I don't need to chase or convince. I become a tuning fork for the room. Others calibrate to the strength I hold.

⚡SWITCH

I don't pull others into flow—I transmit it. I hold alignment so clearly, others feel what's possible. If I want to lead, I go first—with energy worth following.

SPARK 50:

Infinite Circuit

Live in the Loop

You're not done—
You're reconnected.

ϟ CHARGE

An infinite circuit doesn't drain. It renews. Energy flows out and returns—transformed, refined, sustained. Nothing is wasted in a well-wired system. It all feeds the next loop.

ϟ FLOW

When I live in alignment—giving, receiving, restoring—I stop trying to hoard power and start becoming part of it. This is how systems grow.
This is how we stay lit.

ϟ SWITCH

I will stay in the circuit, knowing power moves in cycles. My charge can never be lost — only redirected. This isn't the end of the spark — it's the beginning of the loop. I'm not done — I'm reconnected.

FINAL MESSAGE TO US

STAY IN THE CIRCUIT

We don't just live in a system.
We carry it inside us.

I HAVE THE POWER

Every spark in this book wasn't about adding something new.
It was about remembering what's already wired into us.

We are the conductors, the resistors, the capacitors, the sources. We regulate, amplify, hold, and release. We don't just survive in the system — we shape it.

When we honor our current, clear our circuits, and choose where our energy flows, we stop burning out and start lighting up.

We stay in the loop. We keep the current alive. And we remember: We were born live-wired. The circuit we build together shapes the current we carry forward.

Rewiring Your Blueprint Starts With A Plan...

My Rewired Blueprint

CHARGE

FLOW

SWITCH

My Rewired Blueprint

CHARGE

FLOW

SWITCH

My Rewired Blueprint

⚡CHARGE

⚡FLOW

⚡SWITCH

The Circuit of Wealth

Rewire Energy. Restore Flow. Redefine Wealth.

What if money isn't fuel—but current?

In The Circuit of Wealth, you won't find budgeting hacks or hustle strategies. You'll find the truth most systems won't tell you: money is energy, and you are the power source.

This isn't another book about positive thinking or manifesting millions by wishing hard. It's a grounded, metaphor-rich guide to recognizing how your personal circuitry—your patterns, pressure, and power—either moves wealth or blocks it.

Using the language of electricity and the wisdom of energetic alignment, this book helps you:

Rewire your mindset without self-help fluff

Restore your personal flow through clean energy decisions

Redefine wealth as something you generate, not chase

Whether you're burned out, stuck in financial loops, or ready to finally feel aligned with your money and mission—this book will show you how to plug back in and carry power like you were born to.

Made in the USA
Monee, IL
04 November 2026

67383938R00069